feel the burn

Always Loved Never Forgotten

Always Loved Never Forgotten

LOOK
84

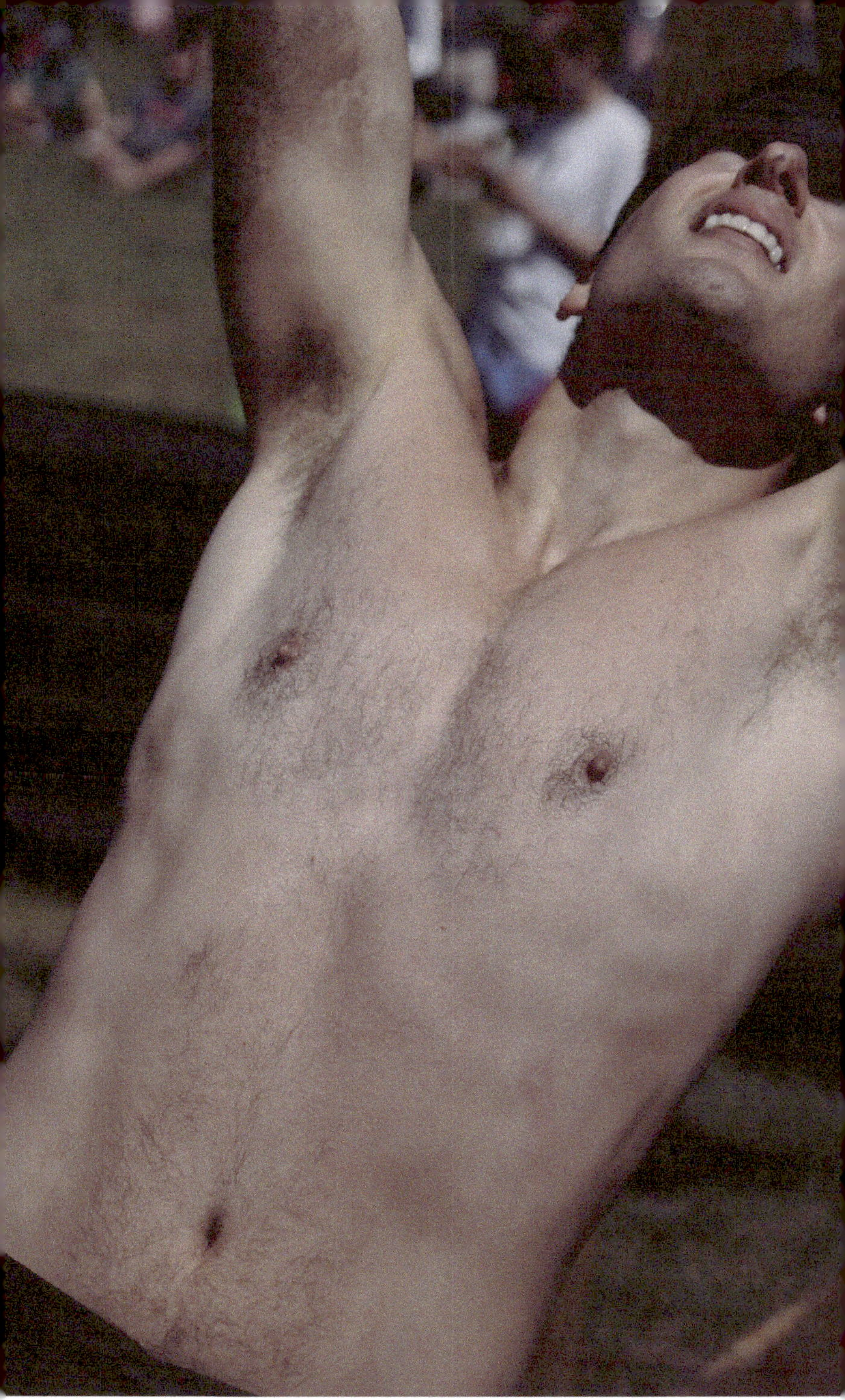

455

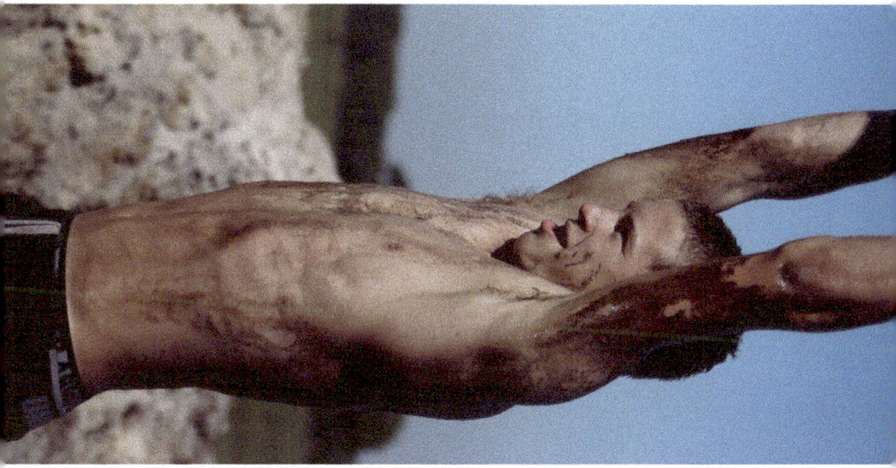

HOG WILD V MUD RUN

HOG WILD

HOG WILD

V MUD RUN

MUD RUN

SEAFOOD

HOG WILD V MUD RUN

HOG WILD
HOG WILD

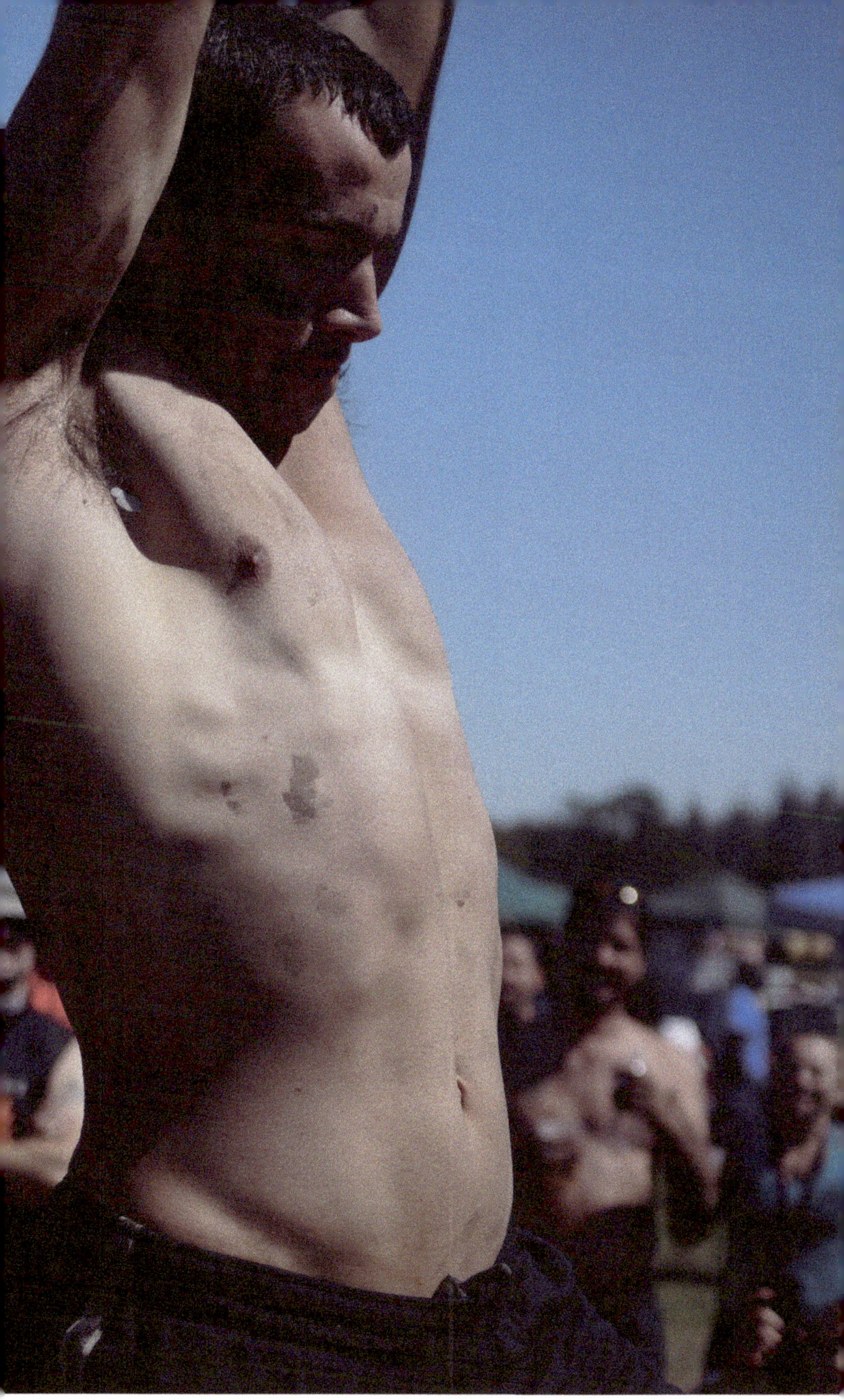

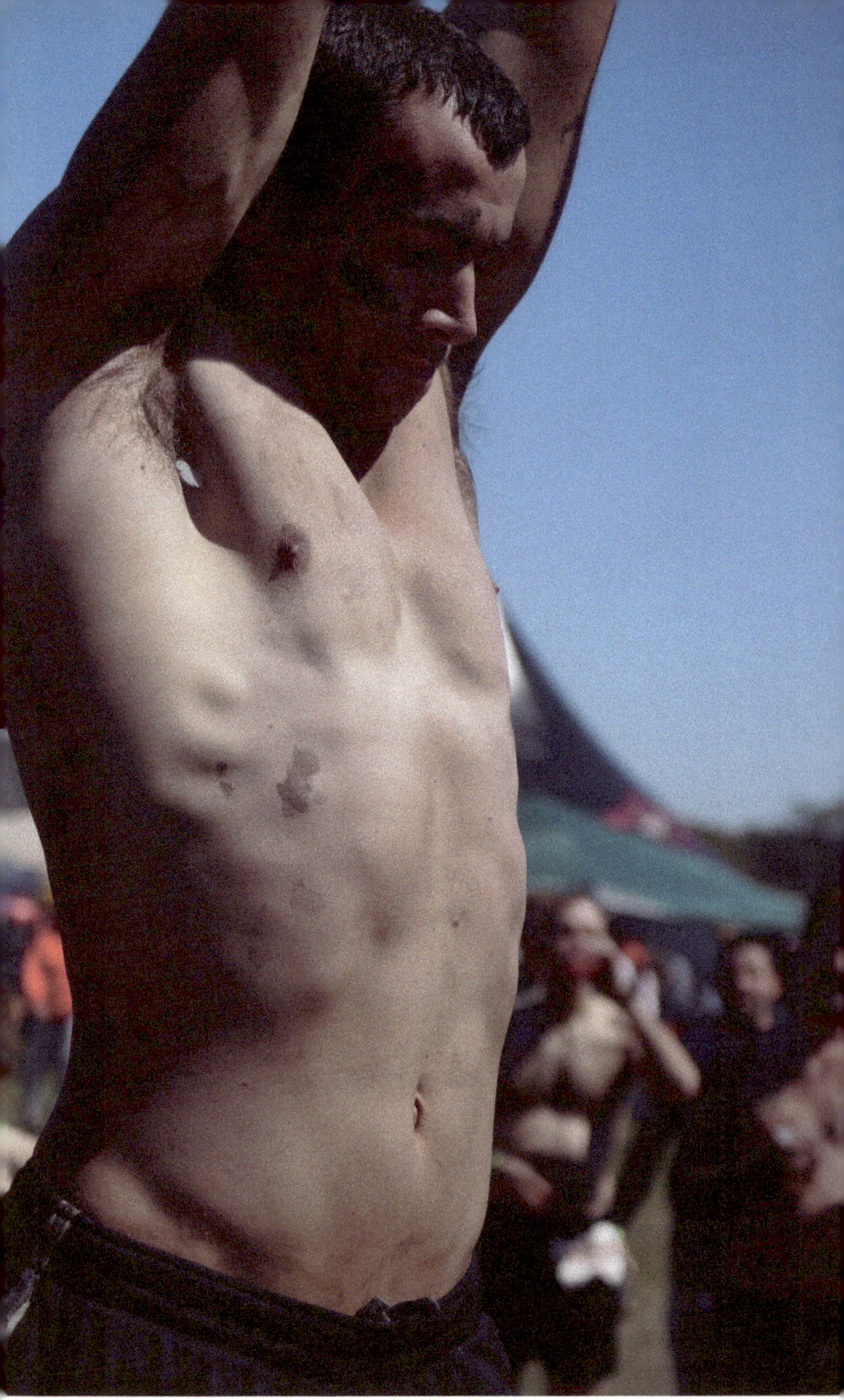

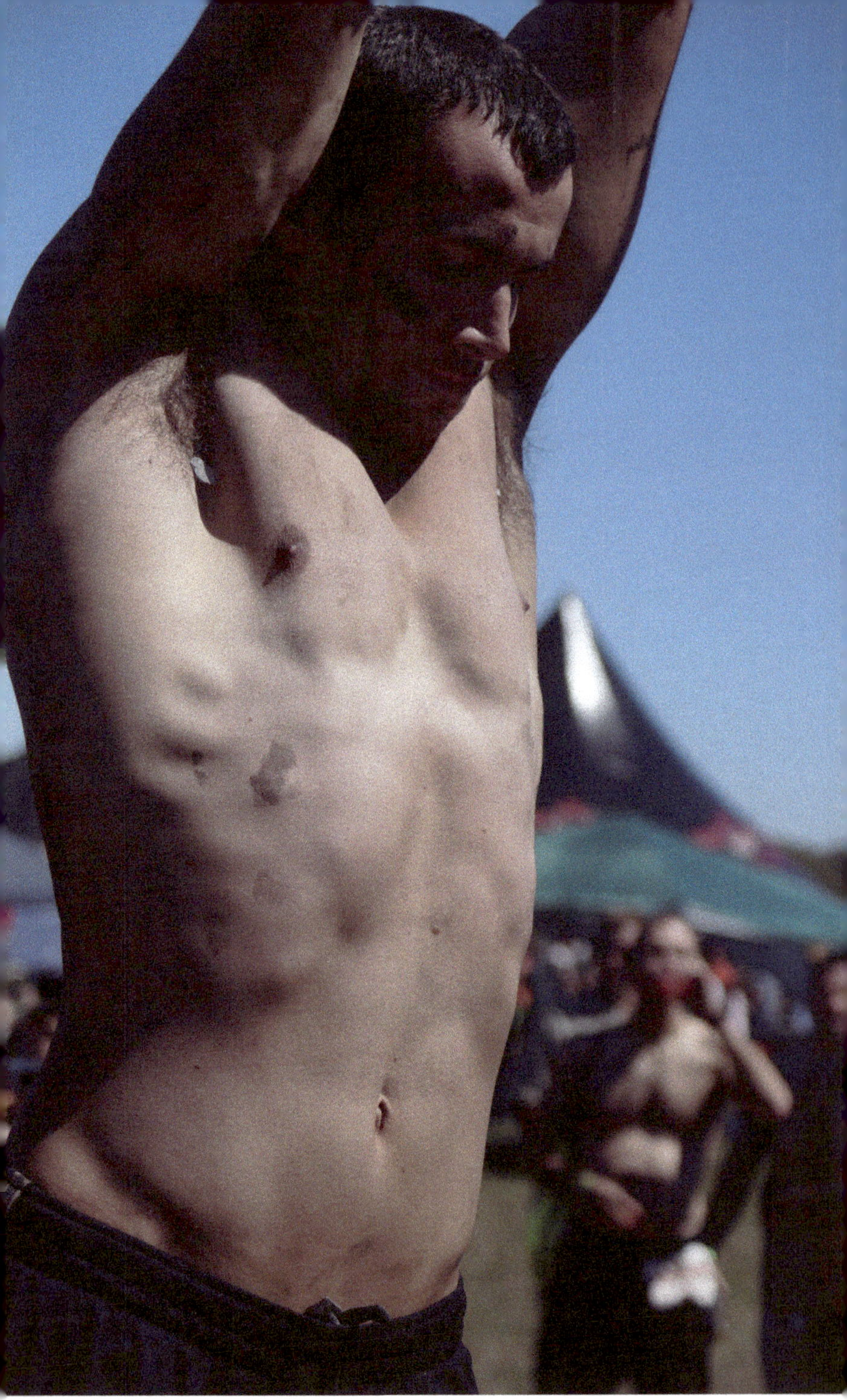

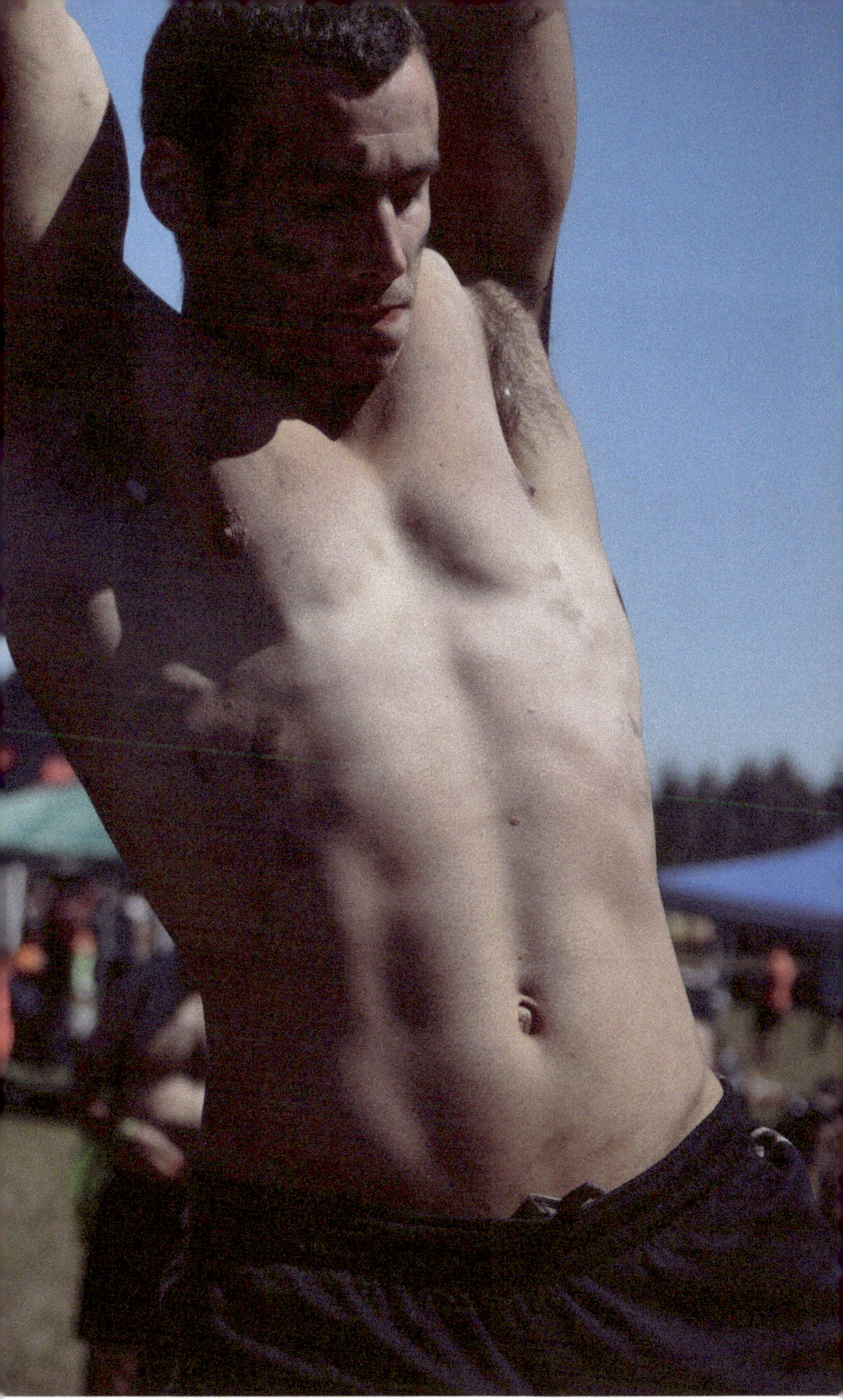

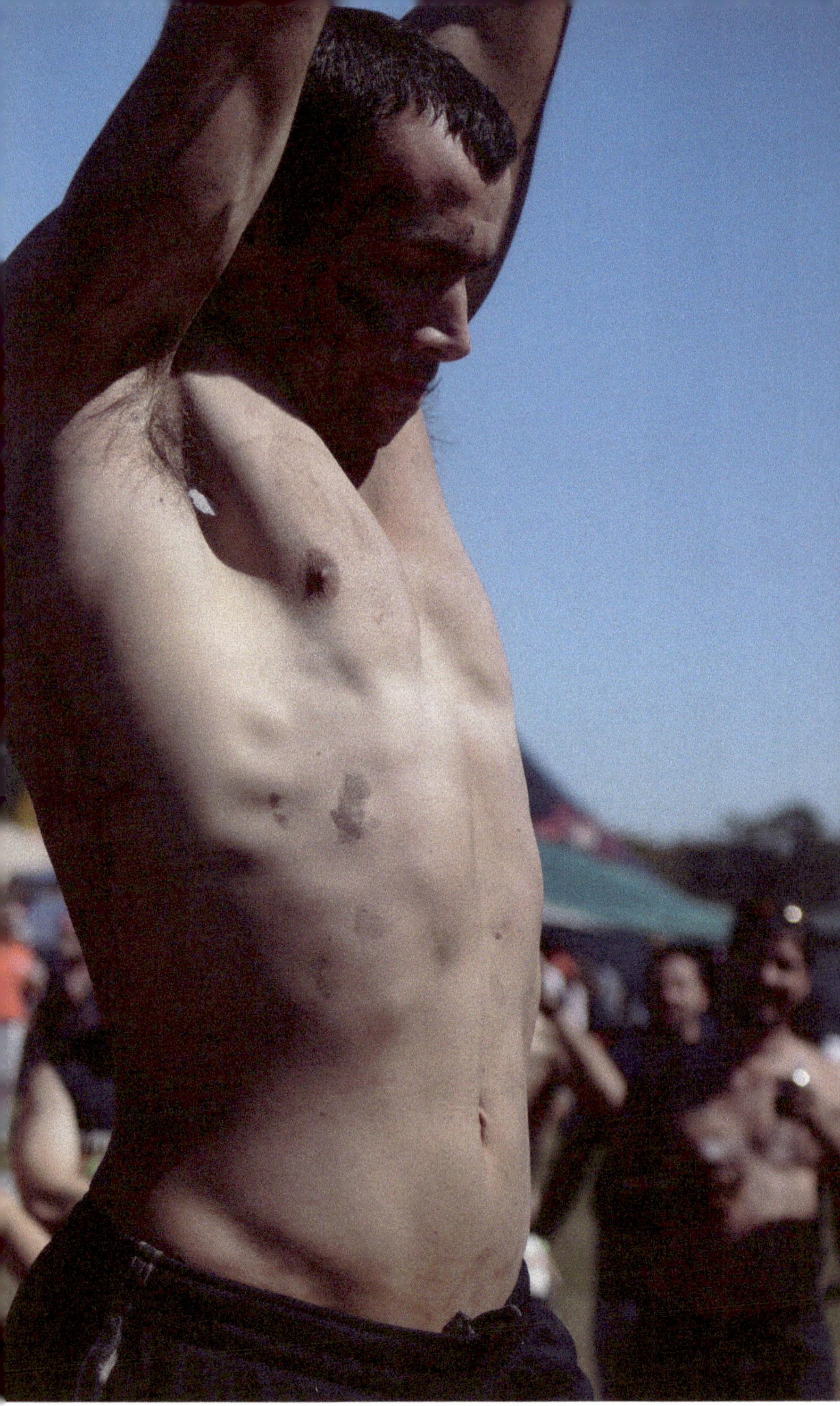

MUD
RUN

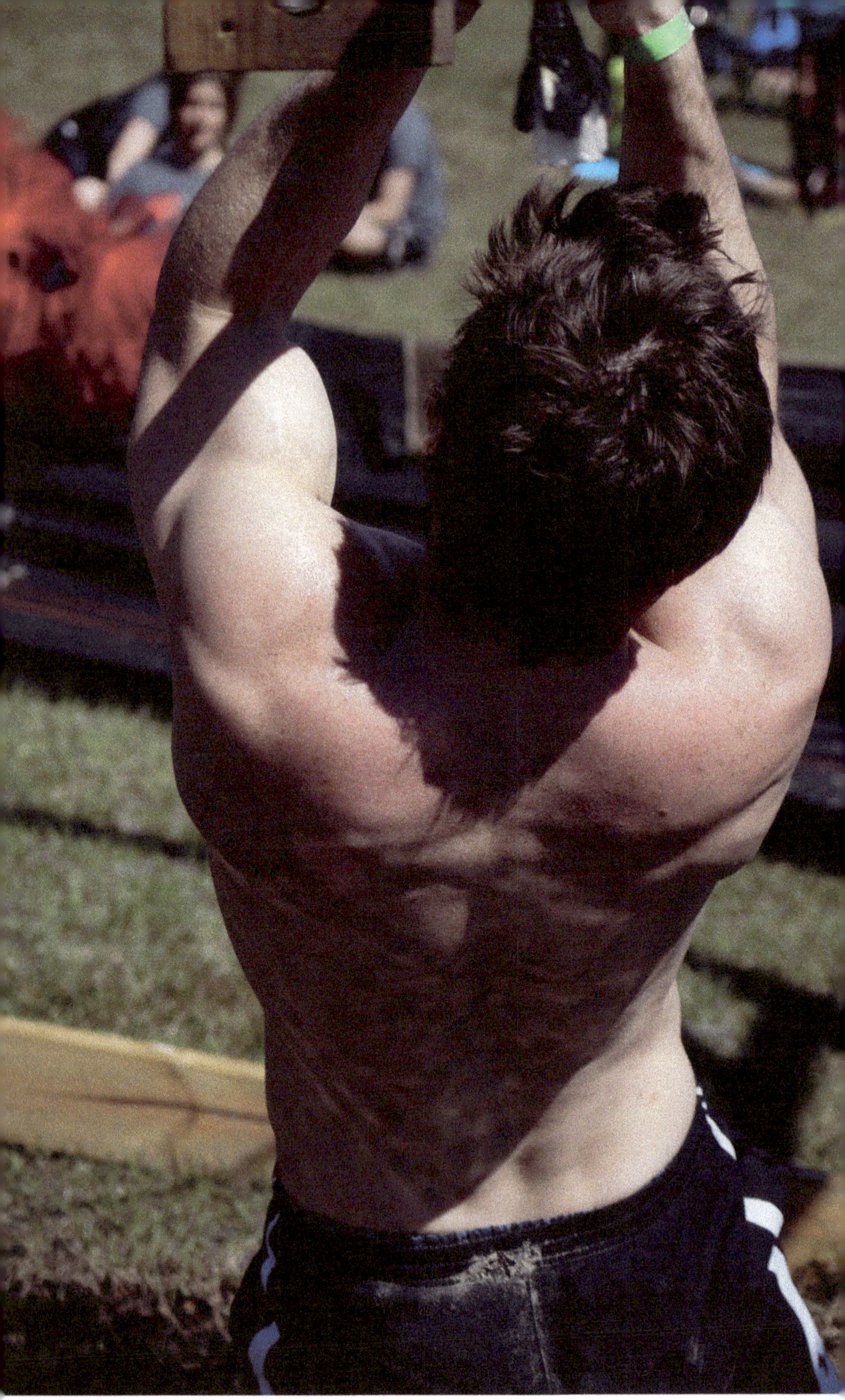

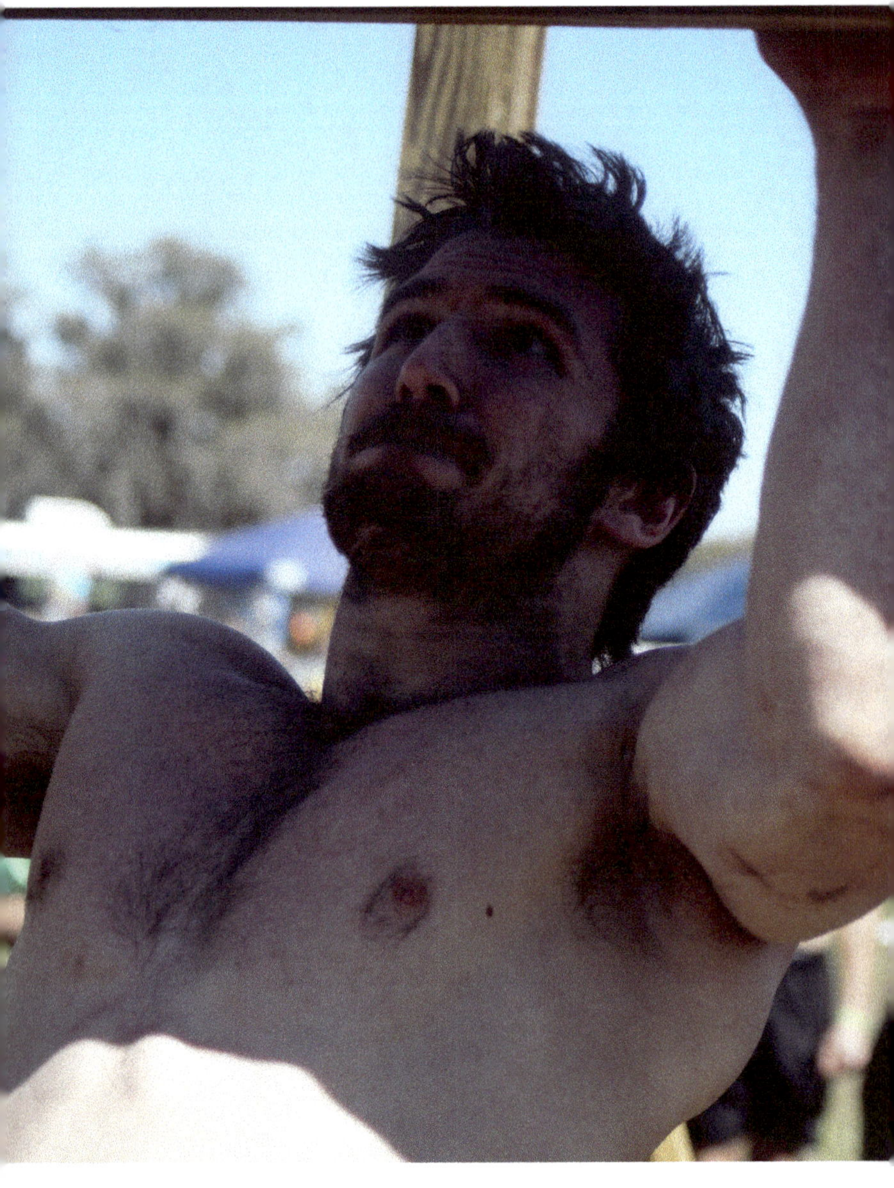

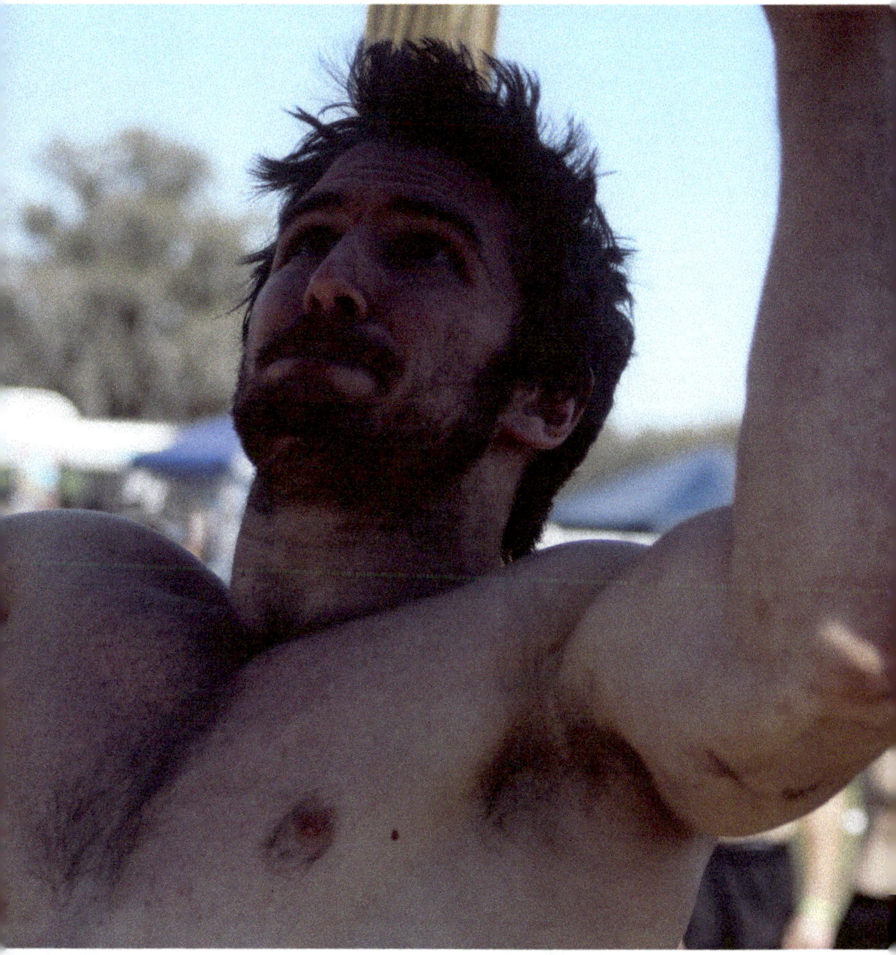

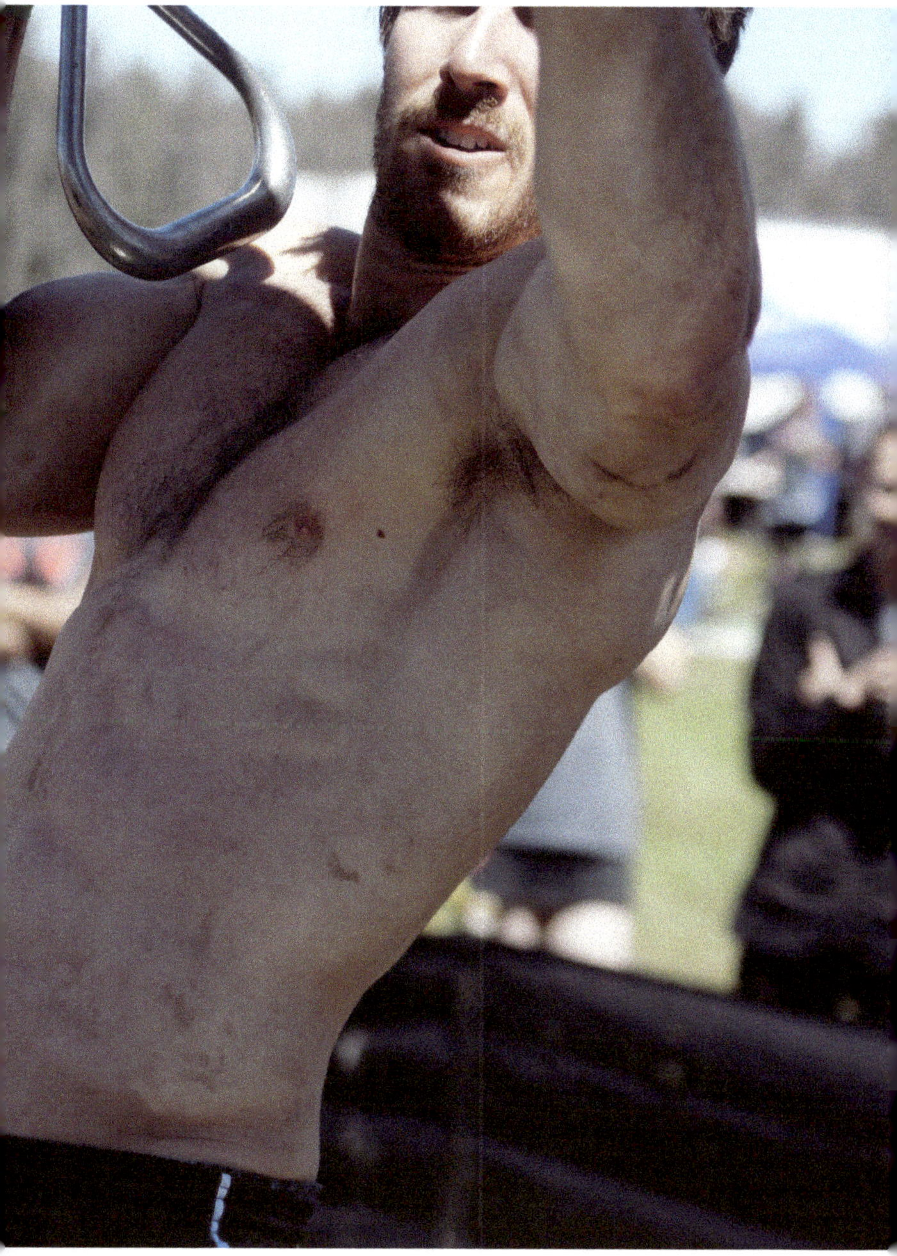

979

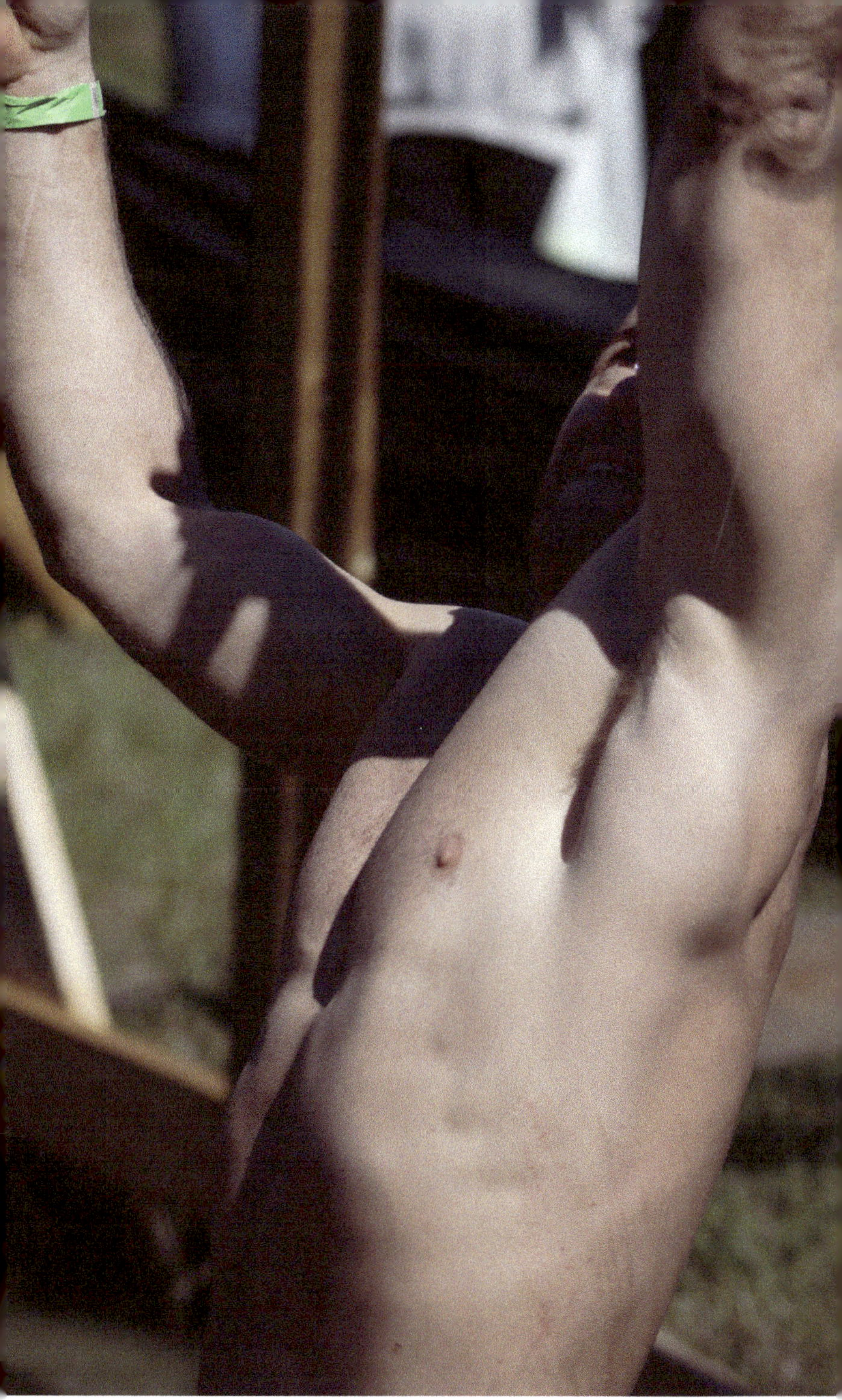

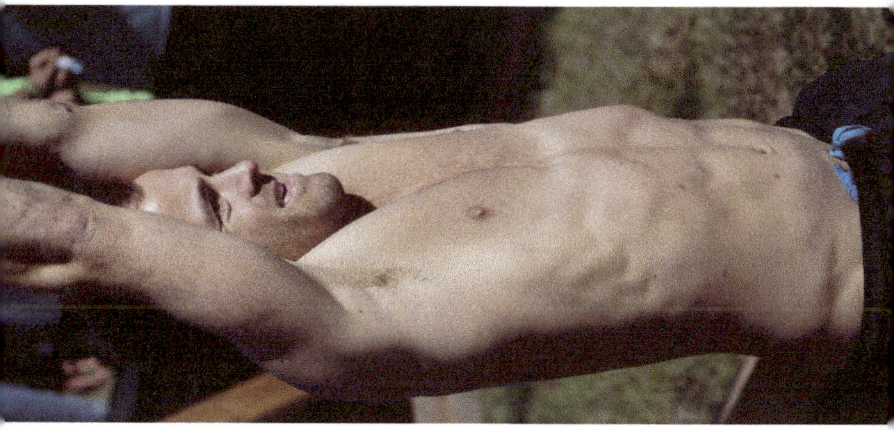

CPSIA information can be obtained
at www.ICGtesting.com
Printed in the USA
BVHW060925060319
541923BV00021B/1035/P

9 780368 363283